The Rescue

Kittie Lambton

Copyright © 2020

First edition.

The author asserts the moral right under the Copyright, Designs and Patents Act 1988 to be identified as the author of this work.

All rights reserved. No part of this publication may be reproduced, stored in a retrieval system or transmitted, in any form or by any means without the prior consent of the author, nor be otherwise circulated in any form of binding or cover other than that with which it is published and without a similar condition being imposed on the subsequent purchaser.

Cover design by Creative Covers. Typesetting by Book Polishers.

ISBNs:

978-1-8381049-0-0 (paperback)

978-1-8381049-1-7 (ebook)

For Gica

Chapter 1

The white light is especially bright first thing in the morning. Drenched sand is marked by oyster catchers who skittle across the broad expanse of the beach, leaving tiny imprints in their wake. The pungent smell of the seashore awakens the senses. On such clear days, this is the time to draw what you see before you.

Iain Fields placed down his folding wooden chair, rubbed his fingerless gloved hands together and pulled down his navy blue ribbed woollen hat to cover his ears. His reddish short hair was now hidden from view. He looked like a young sea captain in his reefer jacket; his six-foot four-inch slender frame, sitting curled round upon his little seat. He lifted his head, fixing his unblinking bright blue eyes upon the headland in the distance before him; the clear mist from his breath lightly daubed the air like watercolour clouds being painted wistfully onto paper. The day felt fresh and he drew in a deep breath to savour the saltiness of the dank sea. Early mornings were really the only time to feel as if you were alone on the promenade.

In the far distance, joggers looked like tiny specks of fluorescent colour dotted against a backdrop of blue grey. Iain's direct gaze only focussed upon sketching the shapes of the seascape before him. He sharpened his pencil with a small pocket knife that he kept wrapped up in an old cloth in his pocket and set to work looking up and down in repeated succession as if nodding his head in appreciation of the sea and sky divide. He had drawn this very same scene since he was a little boy. A creative drive to etch, an inner trait to almost carve out his viewpoint of the world in its ever-changing light.

Katherine Kingsley, who enjoyed walking along the wide-open beach to the left of the panned frame, climbed up to stand upon the concrete wall. She gazed down the length of the promenade. She smiled as she saw the outline of the artist, seated further along the beach, crouched over like a half open pair of dividers. She could just see his pale profile; the navy coat and paint spotted jeans, his white trainers which she knew to be old and worn. The colours of the reddish sandstone from the swimming baths behind him contrasted against his hunched over figure. She tugged against the metal rail and leaned backwards, her long dark brown hair falling away from the curl of the neck of her hand knitted jumper, she herself had knitted. She watched Iain with a happy smile, as he remained fixed and in place as if intrinsically drawn into the built landscape about him by the Georgian architect, who had created such a beautiful setting.

Katherine understood Iain's seemingly endless quest to draw, as if pushing a huge boulder like Sisyphus up the hill before him; never tiring, never stopping but relentlessly needing to move his hands and draw out shapes. She herself was a musician and spent many hours rehearsing and practicing the fiddle, alone in the music room of her home. As a professional fiddle player, she understood that the 'alone times' she had come to know throughout much of her life, were to be savoured moments; the only way to properly focus and concentrate, to persevere through a melodic phrase in order to try to enhance her technique and, ultimately, her performance. She loved nothing better than to watch fellow artists working, even from a distance, no matter their form of expression.

Katherine lightly tapped her foot against the wall; lost in thought. Her woollen sleeve flopped over her wrist and she glanced down, her eye catching the signet ring she wore on the middle finger of her left hand. The solid gold ring had not been taken off since she had received it two years prior. She climbed down from the wall, taking her time to do so, and then rested her back against the rail, twisting the weighty object gently, her hand now hidden from view under her sleeve. Katherine closed her eyes and stood motionless. By closing her eyes, she could picture her brother before her, as if, in her own way, communing with the dead.

A seagull circled downward and stood still awhile, making a sharp squawk before blinking and chortling to itself. Iain stiffened his back and sat up straight to break for a moment from his intensive drawing. He looked down at the bird as it strutted about in front of him, before taking to flight once more. Iain looked back upward to the far view. With the rough draft of his sketch completed, he made the decision to pack up earlier than usual, and head back to the warmth of his studio.

Katherine stood under the cover of the amusement arcade roof and watched as Iain folded up his chair. Iain never noticed her quietly hidden in the background when he was drawing outside on the seafront. Her brother, Jonathan, had loved Iain's work and she had been given a number of his paintings, that now hung in her own home since his death. She liked that her brother had noticed Iain's talent early on. Jonathan had been Iain's secondary school art teacher and had encouraged and inspired Iain's talent, mainly in the run up to his university study and then mentoring as a friend when Iain returned home following his studies. They would go for runs together. There had been local exhibitions, organised by Jonathan, and it was Iain's work that always stood out. His ability to draw would inevitably lead no doubt, she thought, to him finding his own voice within the art world.

Katherine had not spoken to Iain since her brother's passing but knew that she should do and would do; it had just taken some time for her to step forward once again. She regretted that her two sons had never really known Iain; they themselves had had such a close relationship with their uncle.

Feeling the dampness in the air from standing still for too long, she sniffed lightly and wiped tears from her eyes. She pulled up the collar of her jacket and walked around the back of the building in the direction of her home.

Chapter 2

The room smelled of linseed oil and was laden with sculptures, paperwork, canvases, cardboard and tins. To a stranger venturing into such a space, they might have mistaken the studio to be a hoarder's paradise or maybe a room that needed to be tidied up by a meticulous hand. Overturned oddments littered the table, as well as an assortment of everyday things that had been picked up from the park or the beach, that lay haphazardly about the place until the time that a whim would clear the deck, as it were. A toy pram was positioned in the corner with a white ceramic pot placed beside it. The sash window did not have curtains. The air was dry, and the familiar smell made it a space that Iain loved to spend his time. It was in fact, an ever-changing space. His prolific output of work meant that the room was, itself, a work in progress.

Iain nimbly crossed the room to the large white table, placing his sketchbook down and spreading it out firmly with his large hands; a wide piece of blank paper was positioned above the booklet. Picking up a thick paint brush, Iain tipped out the ultramarine blue coloured acrylic paint from its bottle. It oozed out onto a silver plate. Taking his brush, he marked out in wide brush strokes, the rich texture across the grey pencil sketch. It was the first time in a long while that Iain was using colour in his work and he stood for a moment in silent pause, slightly taken aback with this rather bold gesture. 'Cadmium red, ultramarine blue, yellow ochre,' he said out loud to himself, as if repeating a familiar mantra. The smell of cut cardboard lingered. The use of acrylic paint marked an unconscious shift in his thinking. Feeling exhilarated, he smiled a cheerful sudden grin which revealed a dimple on his left cheek.

Iain's friend Tom, who lived directly opposite with his parents, had seen Iain return to his flat not long before.

'Right. Brushes down. You and I are going for a wee run.'

Tom understood how his friend could easily immerse himself for days in his studio and found exercise to be the best way to get his friend outside and chatting. Tom looked fleetingly around the room, as he stood by the landing door. He spotted immediately the open sketchbook laying on the table and ambled over to it, taking care not to knock over an African sculpture that was standing in the middle of the room.

'Good to see you using colour again,' Tom said, behind his warm smile. Iain stood relaxed with his svelte frame leaning lightly against the wall.

Tom MacLeod had been friends with Iain since his family had moved down from Scotland about seven years before. In recent times, they chummed each other on runs almost daily. It was a silent, unspoken release for them both. Iain, twenty-five years old, with a self-assured intensity about him and an ambition to pursue an art lecturing career had only, as yet, been offered part-time work that had barely sustained him. He did shift work, on and off, in a nearby warehouse in the evenings and quite enjoyed the friendly banter with the other men that worked there. The two friends resembled close brothers and were often mistaken as being such by the older folk in the community who would call out, waving from across the street at a bus stop, mixing up their names.

Tom, twenty-three years old, had been a mechanic since leaving school. He hoped that it would not be too long before he could save enough money to move into his own flat. He did not mind staying at home really; he had everything there, including a well-equipped workshop in the garage and his mum cooked his dinners and prepared delicious packed lunches for him to take to his work. In the words of his mother, Tom was 'quite cheeky' at times. He was hard working and had a great sense of humour.

Tom's Scottish grandmother, Mary, who had moved down to Westgate some three years earlier to be nearer the family, would often say to him with a wry smile, 'What's for you, won't go by you.' She relished her grandson fixing things and helping in the house, dropping round almost daily, and taking the time to spend with her. He would stroke her old ginger cat, named Tilly, as he rocked on her rocking chair, quietly listening to her blethering as she busied herself about the kitchen. She knew that his hard work ethic, agility, energy to get things done and, above all, she thought, the kind nature of her grandson, would hold him in good stead for a happy life. Kindness was the quality she most valued and she saw this trait in both of the young men when they often stopped by together, just turning up on a morning, for a cup of tea. They shared their ideas and passions with her in their rumble tumble, sibling-like way whilst languishing like large lion cubs on her living room sofas. Their playful chatter, quietly reassuring and warming alongside the comforting sound of Scottish folk music that she would play softly to remind her of her childhood home.

Once a week, Tom and Iain helped out in the local supermarket, making up food boxes for the older people in the community and delivering them to their doorsteps. They would step back in a respectful manner, smiling and half bowing like gracious soldiers before they went on to the next house, giving a little extra time for the grateful neighbours to wave from their windows and for them to wave back.

That afternoon, with legs like springs, the two young men turned the corner of Carlton Rise and jogged out along the seafront. They picked up their pace. As they ran in tandem, Iain looked out to sea as they neared Margate. He saw a sailing boat he had not seen before anchored slightly offshore in Westbrook Bay and he observed it with his blue-eyed stare until they had turned the corner onto Rowena Road.

Chapter 3

Iain awoke early the next morning. He lay for a time with his eyes closed, listening to the waves outside crashing against the shore. The sash window, at the foot of his old wooden bed, was often left open an inch or two, so as to hear the morning cackling call of the seagulls and to judge the weather from inside. A heavy sea was whipping up. He sat bolt upright and dressed quickly. His usual routine.

'No clear sky today,' Iain murmured to himself. Taking his gloves from the radiator in the hall, a hat from the coat rack and his heavy jacket, he did not hesitate to be outside, blasted by the fresh northerly wind from the beach. He walked down the lane, weather shielded by the houses, until he turned the corner that led him out onto the promenade. The striking headwind made him squint his eyes. He tucked his hands into his pockets and, with his head down, set off on a walk towards Margate. As he approached the harbour, the yacht he had spotted the previous day was dried out at low tide alongside the harbour wall. It looked brand new, but her lines gave her age away. He approached for a closer inspection.

'Ouch,' exclaimed the skipper. He had hurt his finger as he had tried to fix something.

'She's a fine boat,' Iain called out. A middle-aged man, stocky in build, was aboard, fixing a shackle to the end of the main halyard. Iain cheerfully grinned, 'do you need a hand?'

'That's good of you, I'm trying to get the rigging sorted before taking her out again. Do you think you can hold up the boom whilst I attach the vang?' The skipper proceeded to loosen a contraption of rope and pulleys and attached it to the aluminium boom that Iain was now propping up.

'I'm Jim by the way.'

Iain, in turn, introduced himself. The two men shook hands over the boom.

'I'm trying to get the old girl back to her former glory. It's taken some time, but I think I'm almost there.'

Iain helped Jim complete a few jobs around the boat, which was becoming increasingly difficult for him since the tide was rising and had started to lift the boat off her bilge keel.

'Have you just moved here?' Iain asked.

'Yes, from Leigh-on-Sea. I was living there for a few years, living the rat race dream as a salesman. I had some good fortune and decided to give up my job. I am going to see if I can earn a living here, taking people sailing with me as the skipper.'

The two men tidied the deck, placed the cover on the mainsail, stacked the washboards and locked the companionway, before climbing off the boat and up the harbour wall ladder.

Jim Higgins had inherited a Sadler 26 sailing boat after his uncle had passed away two months before. As a way of saying thank you, Jim invited his new friend to warm up away from the sea air with some lunch in *The Heron* pub.

'What'll it be?' Jim asked.

'No, let me get these,' Iain chipped in.

'Not at all. This one's on me, as a thanks for your help.'

'Thanks, a Guinness then Jim.'

'Two pints of Guinness please,' Jim ordered at the bar.

'Take a seat lads. I'll bring them over,' the bartender replied.

Both men sat at the far side of the bar, next to the window, with a view over the bay. Iain took off his woollen hat and rubbed the top of his shaved head lightly. He slipped the hat into the side pocket of his jacket that he had placed on the empty chair beside him. Iain sat forward and folded his arms loosely on the table. He gave Jim his full, undivided attention, warmly looking directly into his eyes.

Jim wore a measured expression. He had skippered boats for a number of years on and off, taking boats for summer sails and training crew for sailing qualifications and the like. He was well liked by other men. He was a good mentor with an innate patience about him; an excellent listener with an inherent instinct to quietly step in and take over in any given situation, always in a modest, caring and understated type of way. A natural leader.

Jim leaned back on his chair and reached over to pull up two menus, handing one to Iain. Both men smiled at each other and then looked over the menu in quiet contemplation. Already there was an affinity between them. A connection somehow. Iain placed the menu back on the metal stand, and rested his hands upon the table, just as the barman arrived with their drinks.

'Grand job,' Jim announced, as the two pints were placed on bar mats before them.

'I'll have the battered cod and chips please.'

Iain nodded and smiled, 'same for me, Jack,' and signalled toward his friend.

'This is Jack. Jackie, Jim.' The two men shook hands.

'Good to meet you. Welcome to Westgate,' Jack said, cheerful in his work.

'So, what brought you here Jim?' Iain asked.

Jim supped at his Guinness before responding. 'My Uncle Charlie lived in Margate and, as a boy, I would come here for my summer holidays. We used to sail the boat together and that's when he taught me how to sail. He was a Lecturer in Archaeology at the University of Canterbury. After I started working as a salesman, travelling around the country, with my base in Leigh-on-Sea, I didn't really see much of him. When my father died a couple of years ago, I reconnected with my uncle and learned that he had been suffering from arthritis for a number of years. We talked about the old sailing days and I said to him, why don't we restore *Madeline?* He had kept her in a yard not far from here and when I saw her, I thought it would be a great project to bring her back from her pretty sorrowful state and get her fixed up. My plan was to get Charlie back out on the water, particularly in the summer months, which I knew he would absolutely love. He was great. I would take him to the yard, and he advised me about the restoration work and kind of guided me through the process.'

'You've done a great job on her. *Madeline* is a great name for a boat,' Iain remarked, before drinking from his pint glass.

'I was coming over most weekends, as you can imagine, to see Charlie and work on the boat. I spent every free moment I had getting *Madeline* back to her former glory. The deeply sad part of this is that Uncle Charlie died just before I managed to finish the work, so he never got to go out on her and see her in her full glory.' Jim's eyes were misty when he looked up and Iain leaned forward, reaching out his arm, placing his hand on Jim's shoulder. Both men sat together in silence, but for the quiet chatter from across the bar, and the gentle hum from the television in the far room which was turned on at a very low volume. Jim looked out at the sea, turning his head toward the direction of *Madeline.*

Jim sipped his Guinness and looked back at Iain with mournful eyes. 'I was surprised to learn that I was the only beneficiary of Uncle Charlie's estate. I had been left his house here in Margate, quite substantial savings, the yard and of course, *Madeline*.' Jim's voice faltered a little. 'Uncle Charlie knew how much I loved this boat.' Jim looked up. His dark brown eyes glistened. 'He was right there.'

Both men finished eating their hot food, taking their time. Jim raised his hand to signal paying the bill and both men stepped out into the late afternoon sun, walking slowly towards the yacht.

Chapter 4

Katherine lived in a gorgeous, spacious, stone walled terraced house which had a community bowling green, beyond the garden wall, at the back. During the summer months, you could sit in the kitchen with the sash window wide open with large cushions about you. Orange and yellow nasturtium and red, white and pink geraniums were placed on the windowsill outside. Reading by the window whilst listening to the quiet tap of the bowls as the games played out below were a summertime preoccupation. At the front entrance of the house, there was a door which led onto a sweeping stone staircase.

As you stepped into the homely house, you were immediately met by a serene warmth. There was a sense of bohemian heritage and culture about the place. There were bookshelves aplenty, old framed photographs of family members with bright- eyed children holding fiddles and cellos hanging on the walls. A Syrian rug adorned the hallway leading into a pure white painted bedroom which had a large white wooden bed, white duvet, blankets and sheets. The view looked out upon charcoal grey rooftops through the huge sash window. Children could be heard playing in the road below. They cycled up and down and played curby against the pavement; running about with joy and carefree delight.

A large avocado tree was the only feature in the bedroom and a stack of well-read books lay on the floor by the bed. The music room, which was on the opposite side of the hall was also a spare bedroom, dark red in colour, with a raised bed on stilts all the way up to the tall ceiling. The front sitting room was a room for tranquillity and peacefulness by day; a space to sit and rest with pale coloured chairs and sofas, a cream carpet and old looking instruments made from wood upon crafted wooden shelves.

It was the kitchen that looked over the bowling green, beyond the stone wall. Full of rich smells from cooking and twinkly lights at night with lit candles, crafts and trinkets made either by her two boys when they were younger, or left by the many visitors to the home ready to play with the next time they stopped by. Classical music from the radio drifted out from the window, but never too loud so as to unsettle the bowling below.

As a fiddle musician and teacher, Katherine filled the house with her radiance and colour. Students visited the house most days for their music lessons, enjoying a wide repertoire of folk, klezmer and classical pieces, practiced along with scales and technical exercises.

Katherine's eldest son Ben, who was sixteen years old, was seldom downstairs. He would spend many hours playing his electric guitar, up in his attic bedroom most days.

Nine year old Peter loved showing everyone his fossil collection and enjoyed building tiny boats and the like. He would dart in and out of the kitchen frequently, always chomping on apples or digging into the varied dishes that were left out to cool on the kitchen table.

Coffee on the cooker, a well-read newspaper on the chair and a welcoming smell of home greeted all visitors to the vibrant house.

Chapter 5

Tom called early for Iain the following day, to go for a run as planned. There was a stiff head wind. The two young men turned the corner of Carlton Rise and jogged out along the seafront. They picked up their pace. As they ran alongside each other, Iain looked out to sea as they neared Margate. *Madeline* was moored in the harbour.

Iain pointed toward her mooring and the two men pushed forward against the wind. Iain wanted to introduce Tom to Jim as they had both been invited out for a sail on the boat the following day.

'Hey Jim. How's it going?' Iain shouted out. The men could really only stop for a short while before their legs would begin to seize up from the chilled air and they would start to get cold. They had another eight miles or so planned for their run.

'The wind should be calming down later on and there should be good weather for us tomorrow,' Jim called out from his boat as she bobbed about on the high tide.

'Nae bother Jim,' Tom responded. 'See you tomorrow.' The men waved from the sea wall, before turning and continuing on their run.

Chapter 6

Tom, Iain and Jim set off early the next day. Jim was right, the wind had died down the night before, but remained perfect for sailing. They set out from Margate due East in a mild south-westerly breeze. The boat was set beautifully on a broad reach and cut through the water like a dorsal fin. The offshore breeze and the falling tide, made for calm conditions and the boat sped along, well balanced at five knots. This was the first time that Jim had sailed the boat properly since she had been lovingly renovated. A mixture of pride and excitement was reflected on Jim's beaming face as he steered a steady course.

'My Uncle Charlie was a great sailor,' Jim reminisced. 'We loved going out on this very boat when I was a boy. It's quite something seeing her back where she belongs. Pity Charlie ain't here today!' Jim looked up at the sky, past the windex at the top of the mast, towards the heavens, from where he believed Charlie would be looking down.

Their route was to sail out for approximately three hours on the remainder of the falling tide before turning back. The route home would take longer against the wind, but the tide would help them to reach home before nightfall. Once out into the open sea, the three men hunkered down to chat and relax in the cockpit at the stern of the boat. Iain took out his sketchbook and sat across from Jim who remained on the tiller.

'Do you lads play any musical instruments?' Jim asked. 'I'm

very fond of the fiddle but haven't played in a few years.'

Iain shook his head and Tom replied, 'I play the accordion a little. My Scottish grandma taught me. Do you have a fiddle?'

'Yes,' said Jim, 'I've got one back at the house, but it hasn't been out of its case in years! Do you have any arts and music events in the local town?'

Tom smiled. 'We have music and dance maybe twice a year in the town hall, like Ceilidhs, and *The Bridge* pub plays folk music every other Friday. I'm a bit biased with the Scottish folk music mind, being a Scot and all!' Tom chuckled to himself. 'People go along and join in with the playing. It's good fun.'

Jim smiled and the three men looked ahead toward the horizon. They listened to the sound of the wind and the lapping against the hull as the boat cut through the water.

'Don't forget about Katherine who teaches fiddle in the town. She also runs a fiddle group,' Iain said, squinting, as he turned to concentrate on sketching the shape of the winch. 'She's really nice,' he said quietly to himself, which Tom actually heard quite distinctly.

'And single,' Tom replied. 'Her two bairns must be in their middle to late teens by now. Maybe it's worth getting some lessons again to get you up to speed, hey Jimmy?' Tom swung round and gave a cheeky wink at Jim.

'You'll like her,' Iain said quietly under his breath. He etched finely on his sketchpaper. 'She's nice,' he repeated to himself. Iain leaned forward to feel the rough edge of the jib sheet, wrapped around the winch in front of him.

'We'll have to get you playing an instrument Iain!' Tom joked.

Iain pulled back his hat away from his forehead, and looked upwards with a slightly cringing expression, 'I'll sing you a wee tune next time we're in there,' Iain laughed, putting on a rather poor imitation of a Scottish accent.

The three men enjoyed the gentle rocking motion of the boat, soaking in their surroundings and new perspective of the distant town from the water. A hard worked, tired looking trawler passed them a couple of miles away on its way back to port after a hard night out at sea. Jim brought out some ready-made sandwiches and hot tea that he had prepared that morning and Tom and Iain's faces lit up like twin boys each getting their birthday presents. Iain and Tom sat back and looked up at the small cirrus wispy clouds which softened the clear blue clarity of the sky above them. The men were relaxed, enjoying the fresh air and sense of escape onboard *Madeline*.

Iain looked down at his drawing, and then out to sea. He took out a pair of binoculars to look out at a green and red buoy in the near distance. He admired the sailors for knowing their secret maritime codes, directing sailors safely onward on their course. He loved the shape of buoys, their vibrant colours, a striking contrast to the teal green look of the sea. He pictured in his mind a huge canvas painting with a thick strip of sea and the bold buoy standing like an erected sculpture in the forefront.

Madeline continued on her course. Iain sketched in his sketchbook whilst Tom tested his memory for differing knots with an odd piece of rope he had found in the cabin. He put on some of his favourite Celtic music from the Scottish and Manx band, *Mec Lir,* for them to enjoy listening to.

Raising his head, Jim strained to look at something that had caught his eye in the water far ahead. He had noticed a small object, about a mile and a half ahead of them in the distance. He lifted his binoculars, that he carried with him at all times, to take a closer look and saw a small rubber boat which appeared to be drifting without anyone on board.

'Lads, there's a boat ahead which looks to be very small to be this far out at sea,' Jim declared, and both Tom and Iain sprung up to take turns to have a look.

'We will head over there and take a closer look. Sheet in the sails a bit, while I harden up into the wind,' Jim directed.

As they sailed past the small rubber boat, the three men could still not see anyone on board. Tom jumped up and held the shroud to get a higher vantage point from where he could look directly onto the boat. 'Lads, there's someone curled up at the bottom of the boat.'

Without hesitation, Jim pointed head to wind while Tom furled the jib, bringing the yacht slowly to a standstill.

'We'll come alongside the dinghy to help him.'

Jim turned on the engine and tightened the mainsheet as he slowly circled around, back towards the small dinghy. Tom stepped forward of the mast and lowered the mainsail.

'Tom,' called Jim, 'grab the boat hook lashed there to the handrail on the coach roof.'

Following Jim's command and clear instruction, Tom nimbly jumped across, soon ready to reach out and hook the boat. Jim motored very slowly alongside, and Iain strained to get a better look.

'Hello, are you okay? We are coming to help you,' Iain shouted out. There was no response. Jim gave Iain a short length of rope to secure the boat to the yacht. Stepping over carefully onto the dinghy, Iain spoke gently to the person curled up who he could now see was a man. He was pale and still. The man moved his arm to his side indicating that he was alive.

'He's weak but conscious,' Iain shouted out. 'Tom, pass me over my rucksack.' Reaching into the rucksack, Iain pulled out a bottle of water, opened it and placed it against the man's lips. Quivering, the man took two small sips, too weak to take the bottle in his own hands. Iain placed his hand on the man's arm to comfort him. He took off his jacket and laid it carefully over the weakened man.

Jim had already gone below to alert the coastguard of the emergency. 'MAYDAY RELAY. MAYDAY RELAY. MAYDAY RELAY. MARGATE COAST GUARD. MARGATE COAST GUARD. MARGATE COAST GUARD. THIS IS SAILING YACHT MADELINE. MADELINE. MADELINE. 2GRC MMSI 235132528. MY POSITION IS 51 DEGREES, 24 DECIMAL, 10 MINUTES NORTH; 1 DEGREE, 48 DECIMAL, 33 MINUTES EAST. WE HAVE COME ALONGSIDE A DINGHY ADRIFT WITH ONE MALE CASUALTY ONBOARD. THE CASUALTY REQUIRES

IMMEDIATE ASSISTANCE. THE CASUALTY IS BARELY CONSCIOUS. WE HAVE TIED THE DINGHY ALONGSIDE. OVER.'

On the VHF radio, Jim waited for a response and a voice replied, 'MAYDAY MADELINE, THIS IS MARGATE COAST GUARD. RECEIVED MAYDAY. STANDBY.'

The coastguard confirmed that help was on the way and that they should not attempt to move the person until they got there.

The man did not move from his position. Iain spoke gently to him to try to reassure him whilst bailing out the water in the dinghy. He looked down at the sorrowful and bedraggled soul that was lying in a puddle of sea water as it sloshed around. It was not long before the RNLI arrived.

The sail back was solemn as the men thought about the poor man in the boat and wondered who he was and where he had travelled from. As they arrived at the harbour, Tom was the first to jump off and tie the line to the harbour wall.

'I think we deserve a pint lads,' Jim said. It was early evening when the men arrived for a drink at *The Heron*. Tom and Jim settled down on an outside bench whilst Iain went inside the pub to buy a round of drinks.

'I wonder who he is?' Tom asked.

'He's obviously a poor refugee,' Jim responded.

'But why would he be on his own and how did he get this far North? Refugees are usually found in the English Channel.'

'Maybe he was trying to get away from something and went adrift on the water. Stole a boat. Who knows. He was obviously trying to cross the Channel.' Jim went on, 'he had no oars, no engine, no supplies, so looks to me like he abandoned a larger vessel.'

Iain returned looking at the blank expressions on his friends' faces as he set down the drinks.

'Crisps.' He took the packets out of his pocket and threw them lightly down into the centre of the wooden table. Iain sighed and pondered the young man's fate. 'Poor sod. I hope he's alright.'

'He didn't seem alright when they lifted him onto the lifeboat,' Jim replied, 'dehydration is my guess.'

'So, what's this guy playing at? What's he doing coming all the way here from wherever he was before?' Tom reached forward for a packet of crisps and added under his breath, 'trying to take our jobs when there are hardly enough for us, let alone anyone else.'

Jim placed his hand firmly down on the table and moved closely towards Tom so as to be able to look directly into his eyes. Jim spoke quietly but firmly. 'Tom, you can be sure that the man will have had good reason to risk his life.'

Tom rubbed his sharp nose and looked away and then back again, his youthful eyes alert and bright. 'Look, I'm a mechanic. Not particularly happy in my job. I live with my parents and for how long? I can't afford my own place, and Iain here,' Tom gestured towards his friend, 'can only just afford his tiny studio and living space. I'm just saying that the grass is not greener here. There are hardly any jobs for us. They all just flood over here.'

Jim interrupted Tom's remarks, speaking in a measured yet firm tone of voice. 'This man has pulled himself away from a world that likely was being torn apart around him. He got up and did something about it. If you are so unhappy in your job and need greener grass, then take a leaf out of that poor man's book and do something about it.' Jim took a long sip from his pint glass and waited for a reaction from the two men.

Tom looked down.

'You were pretty nimble moving about the boat today Tom,' Iain said to lighten the conversation and reassure his friend. 'You know your sailing. Maybe it's time to change your career?'

'Agreed.' Jim responded, smiling and nodding his head.

'I'm fine in my studio by the way Tom. I get enough work to pay the bills. I'm getting my applications out to the local colleges to get some art lecturing work and I'm thinking of diversifying actually,' Iain gestured with his expressive hands, 'creating screen prints, maybe murals. There's a lot I intend to do, and I've only just started!'

'Look,' Jim said quietly. 'I was thinking on the way back about *Madeline* and my move here to Margate. I'm intending to start up a small business getting young people into sailing and taking local people out on trips on the boat. It was Charlie who mentioned the idea to me when we were restoring *Madeline*. What do you both think? You have lived in the area for some time. If I bought a few smaller boats, do you think we could maybe start something together perhaps?' Tom looked up. 'I mean, I'd need a hand,' Jim smiled at Tom. 'I'd need a very good sailor to work with me to help me to maintain the boats and run the business.' Jim continued to fix his gaze on Tom.

'That's a really great idea,' Tom grinned, 'I'd really love to work on boats full-time. What a dream that would be! Are you sure this could work?'

'I couldn't do it on my own,' Jim smiled back and looked at Iain. 'Maybe you could design a logo Iain, try your hand at graphic design? Marketing? I know it's not high art but if we get it right, the business could easily grow. Uncle Charlie was really the one who instigated getting me involved in restoring *Madeline* in the first place. He would love to have seen her put to good use and I've always had an ambition of my own to get back into sailing. Anything is possible!'

The three men clinked their glasses together. Jim was pleased to have shared his ideas with both of the men and to feel Tom's keenness.

Later, after a few drinks, the RNLI skipper who had arrived at the scene earlier in the day, walked past on the footpath on his way home. He turned and saw the three men sitting on the picnic bench and came straight over.

'That's a good thing you did today lads,' the man said.

'How is he?' Tom asked.

'Well, he deteriorated with severe dehydration on the way back, so we air lifted him out to Canterbury. He was lucky, thanks to you three. Not often we have refugees up this way. We still do not have details of his journey, but we'll get a copy of the report for our files.'

Chapter 7

The brown leaves whipped up in small swirling circles outside Iain's bedroom window. The hedge leaves rustled from across the narrow road. The sash window was slightly ajar as he lay awake very early in the dark, listening to the waves crashing against the shore just beyond the row of houses near to his home. *From the summer yellow to the mauve purple brown colours,* he thought to himself, picturing hills and valleys filled with purple heather on brown earth.

Iain closed his eyes and the image of his friend Jonathan flashed into his mind, as if standing before him. He was smiling. Strong. Full of life. Happy.

Jonathan loved running on these cold mornings, he thought to himself.

Jonathan had been Iain's running companion long before his friend Tom had taken up the sport. They would run out along the promenade together towards Margate, around Dane Park and up towards Margate Harbour. They would then continue past the tiny fishmonger shop. Jonathan would often have taken his small runner's rucksack to be able to stop in and then carry back fresh rollmops and fish for his dinner, before waving toward the fishmonger and re-joining Iain on the final stretch back.

This was one of the many routes they used to enjoy running together, navigating about the houses and running off road.

Iain missed his friend. He missed his advice and their

conversations, hearing his voice and feeling his paternal warmth and presence beside him. He loved to picture his friend in his thoughts; to draw out the lines of Jonathan's face and features in his mind. Those kind eyes.

Iain's thoughts shifted to the refugee and to Jim's words to Tom. It was time to let go of his feelings of sorrow. Time to move forward and leave grief behind.

Iain sat upright in his bed and stood up. *Today, I'm going to run another route,* he thought.

As the dawn's first light lit up the sky above, Iain stretched his legs on the low wall just outside his home and swung his arms to warm up before his run, inhaling deep breaths of the fresh sea air as he did so. He had decided that he was going to go for a long run today. Alone. He wanted to take the time to think and find comfort within his own thoughts. He set off in a different direction to the way he normally started his runs, allowing his legs, not his head, to take him where they wished to go.

A sense of release; a sudden lightness and a feeling perhaps that he was beginning to move on came over him. His legs felt like springs as he crossed the pavement and out into the first light of the day.

Chapter 8

Katherine made herself coffee from the stove and some scrambled eggs. She read part of an out of date newspaper from the week before, and sat with her back to the kitchen window, next to the warmth of the radiator that was beside the kitchen table. This was the perfect time of day to do some practice before the boys got up. She always believed the walls to be thick enough for the neighbours not to ever mind. Unbeknown to Katherine, they could hear her morning music practice every day, but never minded.

Katherine stood and picked up her fiddle to play the Klezmer tune, *Gasn Nign*. She would be playing at an event the following month, so she was remembering each of the pieces, tapping her foot gently to the beat. As she played, she turned to look out of the kitchen window and just as she did so, she saw Iain's fast moving figure running in the centre of the road, towards the house parallel to the wall of the bowling club. She gasped for a split moment, half expecting her brother to run out from behind him. It had been a long time since Iain had run this way, not since Jonathan had died. She instinctively rushed forward to open the large window to call out. Iain looked up, seeing the movement of the window, squinting against the light and waved his hand. Iain's legs, towards the end of his run, took him right up to the top of Katherine's stone stairwell, towards her front door. He looked onto the metal door knock, shaped like a fiddle, and stood panting with the sweat suddenly rushing down the sides of his eyes and cheek bones. He wiped his forehead with his hand and rubbed his chin on his shoulder. Katherine's footsteps could be heard lightly as she moved towards the entrance from inside.

Katherine slid the heavy bolt across and opened the door. Iain looked down upon her, his long loving arms reaching out to wrap gently around her, pulling her close.

'Back on the old circuit Katherine,' Iain said, slightly out of breath.

The air was filled with the sweet smell of his fresh sweat and saltiness. They stood together hugging for a short while and then he stepped back, lightly kissing her on her cheek. Katherine led him into the familiar smell of her home, turning away to go into the kitchen. Iain stayed back for a moment and gently touched the key hook, shaped like a key that had been made by Jonathan, and had been fixed by him to her wall. This had been the first time he had been back inside the house, which Jonathan had loved so much. He took a deep breath in and looked down at the array of boots and shoes, a tell-tale sign of a busy family home.

'Would you like some coffee?' Katherine called out from the kitchen.

'No thank you. A pint of water would be good thanks.' Iain stood in the kitchen doorway and watched Katherine as she flitted about the kitchen sink and sideboard, grabbing a mug and glass, and rummaging for a small snack. Her dark brown hair was bunched high up from her neck; her fine dark pink cotton dress, with its tiny yellow flowers about the hem, matched the vibrant glow she exuded as she bounded about topping up her mug with freshly poured coffee. Iain sat down at the kitchen table and examined a small collection of pebbles that had been brought in from the beach.

'I should have come before,' Iain said. 'I'm sorry I didn't.'

'It's fine,' Katherine replied, reaching out towards him, and placing a porcelain bowl and glass before him. Iain noticed Jonathan's heavy ring on her left finger and smiled.

'How on earth do you play fiddle with that thing on?'

'With great difficulty actually, but I'm never taking it off,' she smiled back, sitting down on her cushioned seat. 'I hear you've been sailing. I've seen a new boat moored in the harbour. I was walking past the other day. Was it Tom, scrubbing the deck? I've seen the boat sailing out in the bay quite a lot over the last few weeks, when I've been out for walks.'

'Yes, it's Tom, he's decided to work on *Madeline* with Jim who owns her. Jim's hoping to get another boat to start a sailing business going. He has offered Tom a job helping run the boats for people to go out on. Day trips and the like.'

'Oh, that's wonderful,' Katherine said, 'I thought Tom worked as a mechanic?'

'He's hoping to completely give that job up. He's always loved to sail, so meeting Jim has been great.' Iain rearranged the pebbles into a different order. 'How are the boys? They must be all grown up!'

'They're doing good. Ben was asking about the boats the other day. He'd love for Tom to take him out!'

Iain beamed. He took a large sip of water from the glass. 'So how have you been Katherine?'

'I'm fine. My two young men keep me busy and sane. I'm teaching again.' She shrugged her shoulders. 'I'm okay.'

'Are you still playing at *The Bridge* with your band?'

'Yes, they're the tunes I'm practicing just now.' She picked up her fiddle that had been placed on the window seat cushions and played him a little tune.

'Sounding good,' Iain said, 'Jim plays the fiddle. He's looking to refresh his fiddle playing. I've suggested he gets some lessons with you.' Katherine smiled, hugging her fiddle towards her.

Slightly restless to get showered and freshened up, Iain stood up. 'Right then,' he declared, walking towards the kitchen door.

'Iain,' Katherine called out, stepping towards him.

'Next Friday, bring your friends here, seven thirty. I'll have some food prepared and drinks. Ben and I will play some music. Tell Tom to bring his accordion along and Mary to bring hers too, and please bring Jim.'

Iain turned and smiled his dimple cheeked smile and flashed his striking blue eyes at her.

'That'll be lovely. I'll spread the word. Just like old times,' Iain said, grinning. Katherine smiled back. Iain left and, as the door closed behind him, Katherine continued her practice in the kitchen. She looked out of the window and watched Iain as he lightly jogged along the middle of the street once more. He lifted his hand without looking back just before turning the corner and out of view, knowing she would be watching from the window. Katherine stopped playing and stood for a while hugging her fiddle. She remained still, as she looked out.

Chapter 9

The following Friday, Mary and Tom were the first to arrive together at Katherine's home. They were greeted at the door by her eldest son Ben who led them through to the kitchen where Katherine and her younger son, Peter were putting the finishing touches to the strawberry pavlova.

'Oh Mary, you shouldn't have,' Katherine said. Mary held out a tray of biscuits.

'I baked this shortbread this morning! I thought I would bring a little touch of Scotland to this happy home. And look at your boys, all grown up and helping you in the kitchen.' She squeezed Peter's cheek, and he squirmed, a little embarrassed.

'I've brought my accordion and Tom's got his too. Oh, I can't wait to play some tunes with you all.' Mary sat down in the rocking chair, beside the stove. She picked up a small boat that Peter had made. 'Oh, look at this small wooden boat. The detail. Isn't it so well made. I love the wee sails.' Peter grinned happily.

As the food was laid out on the table and Tom and Ben helped with setting out glasses and cutlery, they chatted about Katherine's teaching and the gigs she had lined up locally. Her fiddle group had been running for a number of years and was very popular for beginner players through to the more advanced musicians. Annually, the group would walk the length of the promenade performing their many tunes together for the local community. This formed part of the local music performances held during the Westgate Arts Festival, where musicians from across Kent would perform in the local park and crafts and cakes stalls would be set up to welcome the many visitors. Katherine was the main organiser of the festivities and local shopkeepers would get involved allowing artists to display their artwork in their windows, as well as providing the various venues for poets and musicians to perform.

When Jim and Iain arrived a little later, the night's music performances had already begun. Two neighbours, from across the road, had arrived taking their turn to perform in the sitting room. Tom opened the door to welcome the two men and led them straight into the kitchen.

'How lovely!' Katherine exclaimed as she hugged Iain and was presented with a bottle of fine red wine. 'And you must be Jim!'

Warmly hugging Jim, Mary remained in the rocking chair awaiting her turn to be kissed on both cheeks by each of the men. Katherine reached out her hand towards Peter to introduce him. He shook their hands politely, remembering Iain's face.

'That's a fine sailor's outfit you have there,' Jim said, referring to Peter's blue and white Breton shirt.

'Thanks,' Peter replied. 'Are you the man that sails in the white and yellow boat?' Peter asked Jim.

'Indeed I am!'

'I've seen your boat out a lot when I go for walks with my mum.'

'That's us! Well spotted! You and your mother are very welcome to come and join us for a sail any time Peter.'

'Wow! That would be cool! Thanks,' Peter turned, dipping his finger into the white cream of the pavlova and licked it, before grinning and picking up a small bowl of olives to take into the sitting room. Katherine raised her eyebrows at her son, then turned, smiling at Jim.

'I can't wait myself to tuck into that pavlova,' Mary said as she rocked on the chair laughing.

'Thank you for inviting us tonight,' Iain said, 'I'll show Jim around.'

Iain led Jim to an alcove on the landing and pointed out a series of three framed sketches he had given to Katherine a number of years back, before going part way up the stairs to point out a larger canvas painting of his that was hanging on the wall.

'Nice work Iain,' Jim said as he looked closely at the painting, taking his time to soak in the bohemian surroundings. Iain then ushered Jim further up the staircase to show him two huge canvas paintings that had been painted by Katherine's brother, one of which had been awarded a prize in a national exhibition. Jim looked on slightly bemused at the vast array of artwork, seemingly in every nook.

Whilst admiring the paintings, a tune from the sitting room suddenly caught Jim's ear, 'I know that tune, but I can't remember the name!'

The men hurried downstairs into the sitting room where the guests were huddled around together, chatting, eating and listening to the live music. Wine glasses and a selection of wine bottles and nibbles were at the far end of the room. Iain and Jim helped themselves and poured out their drinks before finding seats to perch upon seeing as the sofa seats were already taken. The fiddle players performed a couple more tunes, sitting in the centre of the room, before Ben picked up his acoustic guitar, joined by his friend Susan on vocals, to perform a small selection of songs against the backdrop of light chatter. The fire crackled and the light from two large candles glimmered from the mantlepiece.

A small long-haired cat named Lucy timidly entered the room before darting away and hiding next to a bookcase. Iain watched her quick movements before she disappeared from view. He introduced Jim to a few of the guests and Jim talked about *Madeline* and the prospect of developing a local sailing business. Peter was in charge of replacing snack bowls and ambled in and out from time to time chewing on raw carrots and celery.

Holding a wide tray of hummus, baba ghanoush and olives, Katherine entered the room and Lucy sprung out from where she was hiding, circling her ankles as Katherine warmly greeted each of her guests. The room was quite crowded, and she fussed over the sitting arrangements, placing some footstools out in front of the fire to provide her guests with differing options of where to sit during the evening. Iain and Jim stood up to politely give up their seats and, as Katherine looked round, she smiled at Jim. Ben tugged at her loose shawl, signalling for her to pick up her fiddle and she called out for Tom and Mary to get ready to join them on accordion from across the room.

Katherine and Ben began to perform *Goldene Khasene* as a duet together and Iain looked towards Jim who stood with a slice of Comté cheese in one hand and a glass of red wine in the other, wide-eyed with a fixed smile, not for a moment taking his eyes off Katherine. Iain chuckled to himself, wishing he had his sketchbook to hand to sketch Jim's facial expression. He looked around the room, crunching on cucumber and helping himself to the delicious tasting homemade chutney.

Mary and Tom joined them to perform *The Flowers of Edinburgh* and the audience enjoyed the bright joyous sound from the two accordionists. Everyone was tapping their feet, relaxed in the good company of friends and savouring the ambience of the evening. As they played, Katherine looked towards Jim and her radiance filled the room. She smiled across at him, admiring his slightly windswept appearance and rugged looks. Her dark brown eyes glistened in the soft light; her long dark green earrings sparkled in the glow from the fire.

Chapter 10

Two Years Later

It had been a long day of summer sailing. Jim and Tom had taken a family out aboard *Madeline* on a day cruise and they had arrived back to the mooring later than expected seeing as the wind had dropped suddenly on the return stretch. Tired from a busy week of sailing, both men were looking forward to packing up the boat and sitting with a beer to relax. Iain always came over to the boat at the end of the week, and they relished sitting on *Madeline* together at dusk to enjoy the gentle banter.

Jim's company, *Thanet Yachting,* was thriving. He was delighted to have found a second yacht which only needed a bit of work and was glad that Tom was employed on a full-time basis now to help him run the sailing business. Jim was especially proud to have been able to use his inheritance to have helped Tom develop his career. He himself was able to fulfil a lifetime interest in being able to introduce others to sailing and the joy of being out on the water.

Iain had also agreed to contribute to the business. He not only created illustrations of the yacht for tourists but led the marketing of the company, developing their website and coordinating the bookings on a part-time basis. Other companies in Kent were expressing their interest in Iain's freelance work which supported him enough to be able to have time to concentrate on his own artwork and give up his job in the warehouse.

Katherine and Jim's romance had blossomed ever since they had met each other. Jim regularly took Katherine and her boys out on sailing trips and she loved to feel the wind in her hair and the sense of freedom to be out on the wider sea. Both her sons were learning to sail, and each were bought Lasers so that they could sail whenever they felt like it on their own without Tom having to always be there. Ben would always sail with his brother to look out for him. Jim's hope was to introduce younger sailors to the sport, so he planned to purchase a number of dinghies to get more of the local children involved. Running a sea scouts was in the plan by recruiting some local volunteers to get the initiative started.

Jim had moved in with Katherine and Tom lived at Uncle Charlie's old house paying minimum rent which helped him save up his funds and remain close to the boats.

Music nights at their home took place fortnightly. The house was busy most evenings and Jim was in the process of beginning renovation of the rooms in the house, starting with the bathroom, for Katherine.

Chapter 11

It was early evening when the bus arrived into Margate. Families were packing up to leave for the day as the town was experiencing its daily exodus of visitors. Children were cycling away from the seaside; shops were beginning to close. The cool sea air gave a refreshing break from the heat of the summer's day.

A young, refined looking man stepped off the bus, carrying a small rucksack. He waited patiently at the bus stop for his connecting bus to Westgate-on-Sea. As he waited, he looked down at the tiny travel tag and held it in his hand reading out the scrawled handwritten address to himself. He remembered the day he had been rescued in vivid detail. Iain had been the kind man who had spoken gently to him. He remembered the caring touch to his shoulder and the relief that he had felt knowing how close he had been to death that day.

Looking up, he took a deep breath and watched as a seagull swooped down low over a white and pink ice cream van scouring the floor for seaside carrion comprising crisps, chips, cones and other seaside niceties.

Ammar Salah's English was very good. During the rescue, he had been too weak to speak to Iain and to thank him. He remembered the intensity of Iain's gaze, the softness of his voice and the tenderness of his touch. Iain had held his hand, and from that moment he knew he would be okay and would be saved. Iain had given him his own jacket and a rucksack which contained a flask of water, some snacks and a change of clothes. Since that day, Ammar had promised himself that he would return to the region once he was better established to thank the men personally who had saved him.

Ammar casually walked about the bus stop as he waited for the bus, and looked out towards the harbour moorings. The sun was beginning to set, and the sea was calm. At the far end of the harbour wall, Ammar caught sight of *Madeline's* distinctive yellow hull. He could just see that there were people sitting in the boat and set off towards her. As he approached, he could hear the quiet banter of men's voices and knew that he had found the people that he was so looking forward to seeing once again.

Chapter 12

Tall, slender with large dark brown eyes and a huge grin, Ammar looked genteel and handsomely elegant as he stood gazing down at the three men. He stood for a short while looking, taking his time as if a prince accustomed to preparing himself for a grand entrance. He watched the men below him, smiling at them. The men had not noticed him, as they sat chatting together. It was Jim who first caught sight of the visitor, whose dark glossy brown hair hung loosely about his face. It was the sparkle in Ammar's eye that first caught Jim's attention.

'I think this belongs to you,' Ammar said, holding up Iain's rucksack revealing his perfect white teeth, his presence larger than life before them.

The three men were uncomprehending. The men remained seated with their mouths hanging open trying to fathom how this man before them could be the man they found distressed on the life raft that day. It was Iain who spoke first.

'You are the man we rescued. I remember that tiny mark on your cheek.'

'You are right. My name is Ammar. I thought I would find you here; a captain is never far from his boat!'

'Oh, my goodness!' Jim said, dumbfounded. 'Come down and join us!'

Ammar clambered down the red steel ladder that was fixed to the harbour wall and stepped onto *Madeline*. He was greeted with lengthy hugs from each of the three men. Ammar joined them in the cockpit. He looked around him, savouring the moment before sitting down. Ammar's voice was quiet and measured. His manner was dignified, and he radiated charisma. He spoke in long drawn out sentences, sharing his love of the English language with its rich layers of vocabulary.

'You found me at the end of a very long and dangerous journey from Syria. I had been very ill with dehydration.' He put his head down for a moment before drawing in a deep breath and looking back up again. 'What you do not know is that I had left France near Calais, but my engine stopped about halfway across. I was trying to start it when it came off its mounting and disappeared to the depths of the sea. I had been drifting for four days. I was so lucky not to have been run down by the many ships in the Channel. Not one of them saw me waving for help. I completely missed the coast of England and the coastguard later told me that I was heading far out into the North Sea. If you had not found me when you did, I am sure that I would have perished.' As he continued to talk, Tom went down to fetch him some hot tea.

'Why were you coming all this way to England?' Jim asked.

'My father and grandfather were wealthy merchants who had, for many years, traded rugs and jewellery. My grandfather was a collector as well as a trader and loved the rich heritage of our country. The beautiful woollen hand-knotted rugs that are crafted by our people, and the gold and silverware that is handcrafted in our country, is so very precious. He knew that when the conflict commenced in Damascus, the art riches, tapestries and jewellery would be lost. Others did not listen to him, but he knew. He set about transporting the objects and had them smuggled in a container to Liverpool to be collected by my uncle.'

Tom returned with a mug of tea and some shortbread.

'We planned as a family to leave Syria and to travel to England. Two days before we were due to travel, having paid substantial bribes to get the paperwork and passage arranged, Aleppo was hit by the first wave of aircraft bombing. Our house took a direct hit and I was the only survivor from my family. I missed the passage and it took me a number of years to be able to escape the country and make my way across Europe.' The men looked on bewildered, listening intently. They were fascinated and visibly moved by Ammar's incredible story.

'The container arrived, and all the valuables are in safe keeping with my uncle. We would like to preserve these delicate tapestries. It is for me to share my Syrian heritage; the art that has been left behind from war and the goods that detail the rich history and culture of my people.'

Ammar reached out his hand and rested it gently upon Iain's shoulder. He picked up the rucksack and pointed to the address tag in the inner pocket. 'Is this your rucksack and address?' Iain nodded. 'Good, I am pleased,' Ammar said with a warm and slightly mischievous grin as he set the rucksack down at Iain's feet. Ammar sat back once again and sipped on his hot tea. The men fell silent once more and waited patiently to hear the next part of his journey.

'I wanted to find you all sooner, but when I started to seek asylum, the Covid-19 pandemic overwhelmed the country and I put myself forward to help, seeing as I am a trained medical doctor. I was very fortunate that the authorities allowed me to step in and assist and help others and I spent many months working as a doctor throughout the crisis. Everything was put on hold; everything put aside to support and help in any way that I could. As time went on and the crisis stabilised, I was then able to proceed with my asylum papers and try to work out where to go from there. At this present time, I am getting back on my feet and looking to gain further work as a doctor somewhere in the UK.'

The three men continued to stare wide-eyed at this remarkable man before them, with such a heroic story to tell. Ammar spoke slowly and with a measured tone. 'If you had not rescued me, I would not have been able to help and save others. I would not be here, starting a new life without your kind gesture to help me. This fine boat saved my life and for that I shall be eternally grateful. My family would be so thankful to see us here together right now. Thank you for rescuing me.'

The men embraced and Ammar agreed that he would stay on in the town for the time being and spend some time getting to know the men. Jim insisted that he stay over at his house with Tom and he was invited to attend the music evening the next day to be held at their home.

Chapter 13

The following day, Iain had returned from a run and was in his kitchen making breakfast when the doorbell rang. When he opened the door, a large van was parked outside, and a delivery man handed him a note.

'Mr Fields, can you please sign here.' Two men jumped out from the back of the van carrying a rather large and long package.

'Where would you like it?' one of the men asked.

'Ah, just through to the kitchen please,' Iain replied. When Iain closed the door and went into the kitchen, he sat down on the floor with the daylight from the French windows behind him. He opened the note.

'Dear Mr Iain Fields, your kindness saved me. I shall forever remember your compassion and care when you found me. Please kindly look after these rather special hand-knotted Syrian rugs that belonged to my grandfather.'

Iain opened the corner of the packaging with his artist's knife and found the most beautiful rugs. He could see just how stunning and impressive they were just by glimpsing the edge of one of them. He sat back on the floor, trying to comprehend such a kind gesture of goodwill.

Chapter 14

Tom and Ammar walked through the winding lanes of the town together early evening chatting about Ammar's adventures. Tom asked lots of questions, fascinated to hear the many stories. As they reached the corner of Cedric Road, Ammar stopped. The sound of distant music carried in the wind.

'Listen,' Ammar said, 'listen to that beautiful music!' He looked somewhat puzzled trying to work out which song it was he was hearing. 'I know that tune, it's *Gasn Nign*,' he said smiling.

'That's Katherine playing, most probably with her son Ben on guitar. That's where we are heading tonight for our music evening.'

'This is Klezmer music,' Ammar declared. 'This music is very close to my heart. I love it!' Delighted, the two men hurried their pace to reach the house and Ammar quickly ran up the steps to be closer to the beautiful sound.

Knocking on the door knocker, Ammar sprang back and rearranged his tie with a boyish charm. It was Iain who welcomed the two men in, and Ammar immediately noticed the fine Syrian rug laying on the landing floor. His jaw dropped as he pointed this out to them, happy that there would now be four fine Syrian hand-knotted rugs to be found in the very beautiful town of Westgate-on-Sea!

As they entered the sitting room, Katherine stood up and

warmly embraced Ammar, welcoming him to her home. As he embraced her, he noticed from the corner of his eye an oud hanging on the wall next to an old bookcase. 'An oud,' he cried, 'may I have a look?'

'Why of course!' Katherine replied, as Ammar sat down on the sofa to begin tuning the instrument. Ben, who was sitting with his acoustic guitar on a small chair softly playing, listened and watched from across the room intrigued by the new visitor and amused at seeing his mother's charm light up the room with her vibrancy. Katherine announced that drinks and a light supper were to be found in the kitchen and that everyone should help themselves before disappearing back into the kitchen. Peter followed on behind carrying a wooden sword.

Ammar was an accomplished oud player and had played regularly in Aleppo before the war. Once tuned, he smiled and winked warmly at Ben. Lightly strumming the tuned strings, he began to play the introduction of *Araber Tanz*. Katherine let out shrieking sounds from the kitchen, before rushing in, excited to join the performance.

Katherine lifted up her fiddle to play the delightful tune alongside Ammar and two of her fiddle students joined in too and played along.

The music continued with Mary, Ben, Katherine, Jim and Tom performing *The Grackle*. Ammar had not heard the tune before and loved it! He enjoyed hearing the eclectic mix of music styles performed throughout the evening and seeing the joy on everyone's faces as they listened to the live music performances.

With the soft light from the candles, the music flowed through the house and the warmth from the fire settled everyone to rest. Katherine looked towards Jim and she beamed at him with pure love and affection. As the night progressed, Jim stood up to make a toast, tapping on his glass with his ring.

'Thank you, Katherine, for bringing us all together once again for this delightful musical evening. You have welcomed me into your life and every day I find myself admiring your kindness and openness to embrace everyone and everything. Your generosity and curiosity for all things is simply, remarkable.'

'To Katherine,' Iain said, raising his glass.

'To Katherine,' everyone toasted.

'When Iain, Tom and I set off on our first sail together on *Madeline*, my passage plan had us heading north of the Thanet Wind Farm. As we approached, I changed my mind and we headed south, where we found and rescued Ammar. I don't know why I changed direction that day, but at that moment something was telling me it was the right way to go. When I think about it now, I realise that at that time, all of us were actually at a fork in the road in our lives. We were all seeking something new or different but we needed a kick-start to make the change.

For a long time, I thought that it was Ammar's rescue that gave us the kick, the spark that we needed; but actually it is much simpler than that. What is clear to me is that openness and kindness will always help us to steer the right paths throughout our lives. We need to embrace these qualities in every situation and at every opportunity.'

Jim raised his glass and toasted once again: 'To the rescue of us all.'